DYLAN FOX

# Python For asynchronous Programming with asyncio

# Contents

# Chapter 1: Getting Started with Asyncio

A synchronous programming is a powerful paradigm that allows developers to write code that is efficient and responsive, especially when dealing with I/O-bound tasks. In this chapter, we will delve into the fundamentals of asynchronous programming, understand how it contrasts with synchronous programming, and set up the necessary tools to start coding with asyncio.

## 1.1 Introduction to Asynchronous Programming

Asynchronous programming is a programming style that allows multiple operations to occur concurrently without waiting for one to complete before starting another. It is particularly beneficial in situations where a program needs to handle tasks that involve waiting, such as I/O operations, network calls, or user interactions. Instead of blocking the entire program while waiting for these operations to finish, asynchronous programming enables the execution of other tasks during the waiting periods.

In traditional synchronous programming, when a function is called, the program waits for that function to complete before moving on to the next line of code. This blocking behavior can lead to inefficiencies, especially in applications that require a lot of I/O operations. In contrast, asynchronous programming allows functions to yield control back to the event loop, enabling other tasks to run while waiting for the initial task to complete.

Python introduced native support for asynchronous programming with the asyncio library in version 3.3, significantly enhancing its capabilities. asyncio provides a framework for writing concurrent code using the async and await keywords, enabling a clear and manageable way to work with asynchronous operations.

## Key Benefits of Asynchronous Programming

1. **Improved Performance**: Asynchronous programming can lead to significant performance improvements in I/O-bound applications by allowing other tasks to execute while waiting for I/O operations to complete.
2. **Responsiveness**: Applications that leverage asynchronous programming can remain responsive to user inputs and other events, making them more user-friendly.
3. **Scalability**: Asynchronous code can handle more concurrent operations with fewer resources, making it ideal for web servers and applications that need to manage many connections simultaneously.
4. **Cleaner Code**: Using async and await can result in cleaner, more readable code compared to traditional callback-based approaches.

Despite its advantages, asynchronous programming does come with a learning curve. It requires a shift in thinking about program flow and control, but with practice, developers can effectively harness its power.

## 1.2 Understanding Synchronous vs. Asynchronous

To understand the importance of asynchronous programming, it's crucial to grasp the difference between synchronous and asynchronous execution.

## Synchronous Execution

In synchronous programming, tasks are executed one after the other. When a function is called, the program waits for it to finish before proceeding to the next line of code. For example, consider the following synchronous code that reads data from a file:

```python
Copy code
def read_file(file_path):
    with open(file_path, 'r') as file:
        data = file.read()
    return data

print("Starting file read...")
data = read_file("example.txt")
print("File data:", data)
print("File read completed.")
```

In this example, the program will print "Starting file read..." and then pause until the file reading is complete. Only after the file has been read will it print "File data:" followed by the contents of the file and then "File read completed."

## Asynchronous Execution

Asynchronous programming changes this behavior. In an asynchronous model, when a function is called, it can return control to the event loop instead of blocking the entire program. Here's how the same file reading operation could be implemented asynchronously:

```python
Copy code
import asyncio

async def read_file_async(file_path):
```

```
    with open(file_path, 'r') as file:
        data = file.read()
    return data

async def main():
    print("Starting file read...")
    data = await read_file_async("example.txt")
    print("File data:", data)
    print("File read completed.")

asyncio.run(main())
```

In this example, read_file_async is defined as a coroutine using the async keyword. When await read_file_async(...) is called, the program can yield control to the event loop while waiting for the file read operation to complete. This allows other tasks to run concurrently during the wait.

## Comparison

- **Blocking vs. Non-Blocking**: Synchronous execution blocks the main thread, while asynchronous execution allows other tasks to be processed during waiting periods.
- **Responsiveness**: Synchronous applications may appear unresponsive during long-running tasks, while asynchronous applications can continue processing user input or other tasks.
- **Resource Utilization**: Asynchronous programming is generally more efficient in utilizing resources, especially for I/O-bound operations.

Understanding these differences is essential for utilizing asyncio effectively in Python.

## 1.3 Installing Python and asyncio

Before diving into writing asynchronous programs, you need to ensure you have Python installed on your system. asyncio is included in the standard library for Python versions 3.3 and above, so you don't need to install it separately. Here's how to set everything up.

### *Installing Python*

1. **Download Python**: Visit the official Python website to download the latest version. Choose the appropriate installer for your operating system (Windows, macOS, or Linux).
2. **Run the Installer**:

- On Windows, make sure to check the box that says "Add Python to PATH" before clicking "Install Now."
- On macOS, you can install Python using Homebrew with the command brew install python.
- On Linux, use your package manager, such as apt for Ubuntu: sudo apt install python3.

1. **Verify Installation**: Open a terminal (or Command Prompt on Windows) and type the following command to check if Python is installed:

```bash
Copy code
python --version
```

1. or for Python 3 specifically:

```bash
Copy code
python3 --version
```

1. You should see the version number printed out, confirming that Python is installed.

## Setting Up a Virtual Environment

It's a good practice to use a virtual environment for your projects. This keeps dependencies isolated and manageable. To create a virtual environment:

1. **Create a Virtual Environment**:

- Open your terminal and navigate to your project directory.
- Run the following command:

```bash
Copy code
python -m venv myenv
```

1. Replace myenv with your preferred environment name.
2. **Activate the Virtual Environment**:

- On Windows:

```bash
bash
Copy code
myenv\Scripts\activate
```

- On macOS and Linux:

```bash
bash
Copy code
source myenv/bin/activate
```

1. **Install Additional Packages (if needed)**: If you plan to use third-party libraries (like aiohttp for asynchronous HTTP requests), you can install them using pip. For example:

```bash
bash
Copy code
pip install aiohttp
```

## Using asyncio

With Python installed and a virtual environment set up, you can start using asyncio. Since asyncio is part of the standard library, you don't need to install it separately. You can import it directly in your code:

```python
python
Copy code
import asyncio
```

## 1.4 Your First Asyncio Program

Now that you have your environment set up, let's write your first simple asyncio program. This example will demonstrate how to define an asynchronous function and run it using the asyncio event loop.

### *Example: Basic Asyncio Program*

```python
Copy code
import asyncio

async def greet(name):
    print(f"Hello, {name}!")
    await asyncio.sleep(1)  # Simulating an I/O-bound operation
    print(f"Goodbye, {name}!")

async def main():
    await greet("Alice")
    await greet("Bob")

if __name__ == "__main__":
    asyncio.run(main())
```

### *Explanation*

1. **Defining the Coroutine**: The greet function is defined as an asynchronous function using the async keyword. Inside it, await asyncio.sleep(1) simulates a delay (like waiting for an I/O operation), allowing other tasks to run while it's waiting.
2. **Main Coroutine**: The main function is another coroutine that calls the greet function for two names, "Alice" and "Bob."
3. **Running the Event Loop**: The line asyncio.run(main()) starts the event loop and runs the main coroutine. This is the entry point of your

asynchronous program.

## *Output*

When you run this program, you should see the following output:

```
Copy code
Hello, Alice!
Hello, Bob!
Goodbye, Alice!
Goodbye, Bob!
```

Notice how the greetings appear before the goodbyes. The program runs greet for "Alice," then immediately starts greet for "Bob" while "Alice" is still being processed. After a second, it finishes greeting both.

## 1.5 Running an Asyncio Event Loop

The event loop is the core of asynchronous programming in Python using asyncio. It is responsible for executing asynchronous tasks, handling I/O operations, and managing the scheduling of coroutines.

## *Understanding the Event Loop*

The event loop operates on a single thread, allowing it to manage multiple tasks concurrently without the need for threading or multiprocessing. The event loop has the following key responsibilities:

- **Scheduling Tasks**: It determines the order of execution for coroutines and tasks.
- **Running Tasks**: It executes the scheduled tasks and coroutines, managing their state as they yield and resume.
- **Handling I/O**: It monitors I/O events, allowing tasks to be executed when I/O operations complete.

## Running the Event Loop

The event loop can be started in several ways, depending on the context. The most common way to run the event loop is using asyncio.run().

Using asyncio.run()

This is the simplest method to execute a coroutine. Here's the basic syntax:

```python
Copy code
asyncio.run(coroutine)
```

The asyncio.run() function handles the creation of the event loop, runs the specified coroutine, and then closes the loop when the coroutine is done.

## Example: Event Loop in Action

Let's create a simple example to illustrate how the event loop works with multiple tasks:

```python
Copy code
import asyncio

async def task(name, duration):
    print(f"Task {name} starting...")
    await asyncio.sleep(duration)
    print(f"Task {name} completed after {duration} seconds.")

async def main():
    # Schedule multiple tasks
    await asyncio.gather(
        task("A", 2),
        task("B", 1),
        task("C", 3),
    )
```

```
if __name__ == "__main__":
    asyncio.run(main())
```

## Explanation

1. **Defining Multiple Tasks**: The task function represents a coroutine that takes a name and duration. It prints a starting message, simulates a delay using await asyncio.sleep(duration), and then prints a completion message.
2. **Using asyncio.gather()**: In the main function, asyncio.gather() is used to schedule multiple tasks concurrently. This function collects multiple coroutines and runs them together.
3. **Running the Event Loop**: The program is executed using asyncio.run(main()), starting the event loop and running the main coroutine.

## Output

When you run this program, the output might look like this:

```
arduino
Copy code
Task A starting...
Task B starting...
Task C starting...
Task B completed after 1 seconds.
Task A completed after 2 seconds.
Task C completed after 3 seconds.
```

This output demonstrates that while Task B completes quickly, Task A and Task C run concurrently, showcasing the efficiency of the event loop.

## Conclusion

In this chapter, we introduced the concept of asynchronous programming, explored the differences between synchronous and asynchronous execution, and set up the environment for working with asyncio. You learned how to define and run asynchronous functions, as well as how to manage the event loop effectively.

# Chapter 2: Understanding Coroutines

A synchronous programming in Python relies heavily on the concept of coroutines. In this chapter, we will explore what coroutines are, how to define and use them, the significance of the async and await keywords, their lifecycle, and how to handle exceptions within coroutines. By the end of this chapter, you should have a solid understanding of coroutines and how to effectively use them in your asynchronous programs.

## 2.1 What is a Coroutine?

A coroutine is a special type of function that allows you to pause its execution and yield control back to the event loop, enabling other tasks to run while waiting for a particular operation to complete. Coroutines are essential for writing asynchronous code, as they provide a way to handle I/O-bound tasks without blocking the main thread of execution.

### Characteristics of Coroutines

1. **Non-blocking**: Coroutines allow the program to perform other operations while waiting for a long-running task to complete. This non-blocking nature makes them ideal for I/O-bound operations such as network requests or file I/O.
2. **Yielding Control**: Unlike regular functions, which run to completion

13

before returning a value, coroutines can yield control back to the event loop using the await keyword. This allows other coroutines to run during the waiting period.

3. **Defined with async**: In Python, coroutines are defined using the async keyword. This indicates to the interpreter that the function is a coroutine and should be scheduled in the event loop.

## *Example of a Coroutine*

Here's a simple example of a coroutine that simulates an I/O operation:

```python
Copy code
import asyncio

async def fetch_data():
    print("Fetching data...")
    await asyncio.sleep(2)  # Simulating an I/O operation
    print("Data fetched!")
    return {"data": "Sample data"}

# Running the coroutine
async def main():
    result = await fetch_data()
    print("Result:", result)

asyncio.run(main())
```

In this example, the fetch_data coroutine simulates a delay of 2 seconds using await asyncio.sleep(2), yielding control back to the event loop during this time. When the sleep operation completes, the coroutine resumes execution and prints the fetched data.

## 2.2 Defining and Using Coroutines

Defining and using coroutines in Python is straightforward. Let's go through the steps for creating a coroutine and invoking it.

### *Defining Coroutines*

To define a coroutine, you simply use the async def syntax. Here's a more detailed look at the structure:

```python
Copy code
async def my_coroutine():
    # Coroutine body
    await asyncio.sleep(1)
    print("Coroutine completed!")
```

### *Using Coroutines*

Once a coroutine is defined, you cannot call it directly like a regular function. Instead, you need to use await within another coroutine or schedule it using the event loop. Here are some common ways to use coroutines:

1. Calling with await

To call a coroutine and wait for its result, use the await keyword:

```python
Copy code
async def main():
    await my_coroutine()

asyncio.run(main())
```

2. Running with asyncio.create_task()

If you want to run multiple coroutines concurrently, you can use asyncio.c reate_task(). This function schedules the coroutine to be run in the event loop:

```python
Copy code
async def main():
    task1 = asyncio.create_task(my_coroutine())
    task2 = asyncio.create_task(my_coroutine())

    await task1
    await task2

asyncio.run(main())
```

## Example: Defining and Using Multiple Coroutines

Here's an example that demonstrates defining and using multiple coroutines:

```python
Copy code
import asyncio

async def task(name, duration):
    print(f"Task {name} starting...")
    await asyncio.sleep(duration)
    print(f"Task {name} completed after {duration} seconds.")

async def main():
    task1 = asyncio.create_task(task("A", 2))
    task2 = asyncio.create_task(task("B", 1))

    await task1
    await task2

asyncio.run(main())
```

## Output

When you run this code, you'll see that the tasks are started concurrently, and the program does not block while waiting for each task to complete. Instead, it schedules both tasks and continues executing.

```arduino
Copy code
Task A starting...
Task B starting...
Task B completed after 1 seconds.
Task A completed after 2 seconds.
```

## 2.3 The async and await Keywords

The async and await keywords are fundamental to writing asynchronous code in Python. They are used to define coroutines and handle their execution effectively.

### The async Keyword

The async keyword is used to define a coroutine function. It signals to the Python interpreter that the function may contain asynchronous operations. For example:

```python
Copy code
async def my_coroutine():
    # Coroutine logic here
    await asyncio.sleep(1)
```

When you define a function with async, it will always return a coroutine object, which can be awaited or scheduled.

## The await Keyword

The await keyword is used within an async function to pause the execution of the coroutine until the awaited task is completed. This is how you yield control back to the event loop. The expression following await must be an awaitable object, which can be another coroutine or a Task.

Here's an example:

```python
Copy code
async def another_coroutine():
    print("Start of another coroutine")
    await asyncio.sleep(2)
    print("End of another coroutine")
```

## Example of Using async and await

Let's look at an example that utilizes both keywords:

```python
Copy code
import asyncio

async def fetch_data():
    print("Fetching data...")
    await asyncio.sleep(2)
    return {"data": "Sample data"}

async def main():
    result = await fetch_data()
    print("Fetched:", result)

asyncio.run(main())
```

## Explanation of the Example

1. **Defining Coroutines**: The fetch_data function is defined as a coroutine using async def. Inside it, await asyncio.sleep(2) simulates a delay.
2. **Using await**: In the main function, await fetch_data() pauses execution until fetch_data completes.
3. **Execution**: The program runs the main coroutine using asyncio.run(), which handles the event loop for you.

## Importance of async and await

The use of async and await allows developers to write clear and maintainable asynchronous code that resembles synchronous code. It enhances readability and minimizes the complexity typically associated with callback-based asynchronous programming.

# 2.4 Coroutine Lifecycle

Understanding the lifecycle of a coroutine is crucial for effective asynchronous programming. The lifecycle describes the various states a coroutine can go through during its execution.

## States of a Coroutine

1. **Created**: When a coroutine is defined using async def, it is in the "created" state. At this point, the coroutine has not started executing and cannot yield control.
2. **Suspended**: When a coroutine is called and hits an await statement, it yields control back to the event loop. It enters the "suspended" state, allowing other tasks to execute while waiting for the awaited operation to complete.
3. **Running**: When the coroutine is scheduled and started by the event loop, it enters the "running" state. The event loop executes the coroutine

until it either completes or reaches another await.

4. **Completed**: Once a coroutine finishes executing all its statements (including returning a value), it enters the "completed" state. At this point, the event loop can retrieve the result of the coroutine.

## Example of Coroutine Lifecycle

Let's illustrate the coroutine lifecycle with a simple example:

```python
Copy code
import asyncio

async def example_coroutine():
    print("Coroutine started")
    await asyncio.sleep(1)  # Suspended state
    print("Coroutine resumed")
    return "Coroutine completed"

async def main():
    coro = example_coroutine()  # Created state
    print("Before awaiting")
    result = await coro  # Running state
    print(result)  # Coroutine completed

asyncio.run(main())
```

## Output Explanation

When you run this program, the output will be:

```python
Copy code
Before awaiting
Coroutine started
```

```
Coroutine resumed
Coroutine completed
```

1. **Created State**: The coroutine example_coroutine is created when assigned to coro.
2. **Suspended State**: When await asyncio.sleep(1) is encountered, it suspends execution for 1 second, allowing the event loop to run other tasks.
3. **Running State**: The coroutine resumes execution after the sleep duration.
4. **Completed State**: Finally, it completes execution, and the result is printed in the main function.

## Transitioning Between States

The transition between states is managed by the event loop. When a coroutine hits an await statement, control is handed back to the event loop, which can then execute other coroutines or tasks. When the awaited task is complete, the event loop will resume the original coroutine at the point where it was suspended.

## 2.5 Exception Handling in Coroutines

Just like with regular functions, you need to handle exceptions in coroutines properly. Exception handling is critical for maintaining the stability of your application, especially in asynchronous programming, where errors can propagate in unexpected ways.

## Basic Exception Handling

You can use traditional try and except blocks to handle exceptions in coroutines:

```python
python
Copy code
import asyncio

async def risky_operation():
    await asyncio.sleep(1)
    raise ValueError("An error occurred!")

async def main():
    try:
        await risky_operation()
    except ValueError as e:
        print(f"Caught an exception: {e}")

asyncio.run(main())
```

## Output Explanation

When you run this code, you'll see the following output:

```go
go
Copy code
Caught an exception: An error occurred!
```

1. **Raising Exceptions**: In the risky_operation coroutine, a ValueError is raised after a delay.
2. **Handling Exceptions**: In the main coroutine, the try block captures the exception when calling await risky_operation(). The except block handles it gracefully.

## Handling Exceptions with asyncio.gather()

When using asyncio.gather() to run multiple coroutines, unhandled exceptions in any of the coroutines will cause asyncio.gather() to raise the first exception encountered. Here's an example:

```python
Copy code
async def task_with_error(name):
    await asyncio.sleep(1)
    if name == "task2":
        raise RuntimeError("Error in task2")
    print(f"{name} completed successfully.")

async def main():
    try:
        await asyncio.gather(
            task_with_error("task1"),
            task_with_error("task2"),   # This will raise an
            exception
        )
    except RuntimeError as e:
        print(f"Caught an exception from gather: {e}")

asyncio.run(main())
```

## Output Explanation

When you run this code, the output will be:

```javascript
Copy code
task1 completed successfully.
Caught an exception from gather: Error in task2
```

In this example:

1. **Concurrent Execution**: Both tasks run concurrently. When task2 raises a RuntimeError, asyncio.gather() immediately stops and raises the exception.
2. **Exception Handling**: The except block in main captures the exception raised by asyncio.gather().

## *Summary of Exception Handling in Coroutines*

- Use try and except to handle exceptions within coroutines as you would in regular functions.
- When using asyncio.gather(), be aware that it raises the first encountered exception from any coroutine, and it's essential to handle these exceptions appropriately.
- Ensuring robust error handling in your asynchronous code is crucial for maintaining application stability and providing a better user experience.

## Conclusion

In this chapter, we delved into the concept of coroutines, including their definition, usage, and lifecycle. We learned how to define and call coroutines using the async and await keywords, and we explored exception handling within coroutines. Understanding coroutines is foundational to mastering asynchronous programming in Python, and this knowledge will serve as a basis for more advanced topics in the following chapters.

# Chapter 3: The Asyncio Event Loop

T he event loop is the core component of the asyncio library, allowing Python to handle asynchronous operations efficiently. Understanding how the event loop works is essential for building robust and high-performance asynchronous applications. In this chapter, we will delve deep into the asyncio event loop, exploring its functionality, how to create and manage it, how to schedule tasks, run the event loop, and stop it safely.

## 3.1 Understanding the Event Loop

At its core, the event loop is a loop that continuously checks for events or tasks to be executed. When using asyncio, the event loop is responsible for managing coroutines and executing asynchronous code. It allows for concurrent execution, enabling I/O-bound operations to be performed without blocking the main thread.

### Key Concepts of the Event Loop

1. **Concurrency vs. Parallelism**: The event loop achieves concurrency by managing multiple tasks that may be waiting for I/O operations to complete. However, it does not execute tasks in parallel; instead, it rapidly switches between tasks to give the illusion of simultaneous

execution.

2. **Non-blocking I/O**: The event loop is designed to handle non-blocking I/O operations. This means that when a task waits for I/O (like a network response or file read), the event loop can switch to execute other tasks instead of getting stuck.

3. **Single-threaded**: The default asyncio event loop runs in a single thread, making it simpler to manage and reducing the complexity associated with multi-threading, such as race conditions.

## How the Event Loop Works

The event loop operates by following a series of steps:

1. **Start**: The event loop is initialized and starts running.
2. **Task Scheduling**: Tasks (coroutines, callbacks, or future objects) are scheduled to run. The event loop maintains a queue of tasks that are ready to be executed.
3. **Execution**: The event loop runs tasks until they are completed. If a task awaits a non-blocking operation, it yields control back to the loop, which then runs other scheduled tasks.
4. **Completion**: Once a task is completed, the event loop can retrieve the result and move on to the next task.

## Example of Event Loop in Action

Here's a simple example that demonstrates how the event loop manages tasks:

```python
Copy code
import asyncio

async def task(name, duration):
    print(f"Task {name} starting...")
```

```python
    await asyncio.sleep(duration)  # Simulating an I/O-bound
    operation
    print(f"Task {name} completed after {duration} seconds.")

async def main():
    await asyncio.gather(
        task("A", 2),
        task("B", 1),
        task("C", 3),
    )

asyncio.run(main())
```

## Output Explanation

When you run this code, the output will show how the event loop manages tasks:

```arduino
Copy code
Task A starting...
Task B starting...
Task C starting...
Task B completed after 1 seconds.
Task A completed after 2 seconds.
Task C completed after 3 seconds.
```

In this example, Task B completes first because it has the shortest duration. The event loop efficiently switches between tasks, allowing for concurrent execution.

## 3.2 Creating and Managing the Event Loop

asyncio provides several functions to create and manage the event loop. While asyncio.run() simplifies running the event loop, understanding how to create and control the event loop manually can be valuable in more complex scenarios.

### Creating a New Event Loop

You can create a new event loop using the asyncio.new_event_loop() function. This is useful when you need to manage multiple loops or when you want to run the event loop in a specific context.

```python
Copy code
import asyncio

# Create a new event loop
new_loop = asyncio.new_event_loop()
asyncio.set_event_loop(new_loop)  # Set the new loop as the
current loop
```

### Managing the Event Loop

Once the event loop is created, you can manage it using various methods:

1. **Starting the Loop**: You can start the loop using loop.run_forever() or loop.run_until_complete(coroutine).
2. **Stopping the Loop**: You can stop the loop using loop.stop().
3. **Closing the Loop**: After the loop has been stopped, you should close it using loop.close() to free up system resources.

## Example of Managing an Event Loop

Here's an example of creating and managing an event loop manually:

```python
Copy code
import asyncio

async def say_hello():
    print("Hello, World!")

# Create a new event loop
loop = asyncio.new_event_loop()
asyncio.set_event_loop(loop)

try:
    # Run the coroutine until completion
    loop.run_until_complete(say_hello())
finally:
    # Close the loop
    loop.close()
```

## Output Explanation

When you run this code, the output will be:

```
Copy code
Hello, World!
```

In this example, a new event loop is created, and the say_hello coroutine is executed until completion. Finally, the loop is closed to clean up resources.

## *Using the Default Event Loop*

If you don't need to manage multiple event loops, you can use the default event loop, which is created automatically when asyncio.run() is called. You can access the default loop using asyncio.get_event_loop():

```python
Copy code
import asyncio

async def main():
    print("Running in the default event loop.")

# Get the default event loop
loop = asyncio.get_event_loop()
loop.run_until_complete(main())
```

## *Output Explanation*

The output will be:

```vbnet
Copy code
Running in the default event loop.
```

## 3.3 Scheduling Tasks in the Event Loop

Scheduling tasks in the event loop is a key aspect of asynchronous programming with asyncio. You can schedule coroutines, callbacks, and futures to run in the event loop, allowing you to control their execution order and timing.

## Scheduling Coroutines

You can schedule a coroutine to run using the asyncio.create_task() function, which wraps the coroutine in a Task object. This allows the event loop to run the coroutine concurrently with other tasks.

Example of Scheduling Coroutines

```python
Copy code
import asyncio

async def task(name, duration):
    print(f"Task {name} starting...")
    await asyncio.sleep(duration)
    print(f"Task {name} completed after {duration} seconds.")

async def main():
    # Schedule multiple tasks
    task1 = asyncio.create_task(task("A", 2))
    task2 = asyncio.create_task(task("B", 1))

    # Wait for both tasks to complete
    await task1
    await task2

asyncio.run(main())
```

## Output Explanation

The output will show the execution of both tasks:

```arduino
Copy code
Task A starting...
Task B starting...
Task B completed after 1 seconds.
```

31

```
Task A completed after 2 seconds.
```

In this example, Task B completes first, demonstrating how the event loop schedules tasks concurrently.

## Scheduling Callbacks

In addition to coroutines, you can schedule callbacks to run after a specified delay using loop.call_later(delay, callback, *args). This method allows you to execute a function after a certain amount of time has passed.

Example of Scheduling Callbacks

```python
python
Copy code
import asyncio

def callback(name):
    print(f"Callback executed for {name}.")

async def main():
    loop = asyncio.get_running_loop()
    loop.call_later(2, callback, "Task A")
    loop.call_later(1, callback, "Task B")

    print("Callbacks scheduled.")

asyncio.run(main())
```

## Output Explanation

When you run this code, the output will be:

```arduino
arduino
Copy code
```

```
Callbacks scheduled.
Callback executed for Task B.
Callback executed for Task A.
```

In this example, the callbacks are scheduled to run after specified delays, showing how the event loop can manage both coroutines and callbacks.

## Scheduling Futures

A Future is an object that represents a result that may not be available yet. You can schedule a Future to be resolved later, allowing the event loop to manage its execution.

Example of Scheduling Futures

```python
python
Copy code
import asyncio

async def set_future(future):
    await asyncio.sleep(1)
    future.set_result("Future resolved!")

async def main():
    loop = asyncio.get_running_loop()
    future = loop.create_future()  # Create a new future

    # Schedule the coroutine that resolves the future
    asyncio.create_task(set_future(future))

    result = await future  # Wait for the future to be resolved
    print(result)

asyncio.run(main())
```

## Output Explanation

When you run this code, the output will be:

```
Copy code
Future resolved!
```

In this example, a Future is created, and the set_future coroutine is scheduled to resolve it after 1 second. The main coroutine awaits the future and prints the result once it's resolved.

## 3.4 Running the Event Loop: run, run_until_complete

Running the event loop is the final step in executing your asynchronous code. asyncio provides several methods to run the event loop, allowing for flexibility in how you manage the execution of tasks.

### Using asyncio.run()

The simplest way to run an event loop is by using asyncio.run(coroutine). This function handles the creation, execution, and closing of the event loop for you.

Example of Using asyncio.run()

```python
python
Copy code
import asyncio

async def main():
    print("Running the main coroutine.")

asyncio.run(main())
```

## Output Explanation

When you run this code, the output will be:

```css
Copy code
Running the main coroutine.
```

In this example, the main coroutine is executed within the default event loop, and resources are automatically cleaned up afterward.

## Using run_until_complete()

If you have an existing event loop, you can run a coroutine until it is complete using the run_until_complete(coroutine) method. This method is useful when you want to control the event loop manually.

Example of Using run_until_complete()

```python
Copy code
import asyncio

async def main():
    print("Running the main coroutine.")

loop = asyncio.new_event_loop()
asyncio.set_event_loop(loop)

try:
    loop.run_until_complete(main())
finally:
    loop.close()
```

## *Output Explanation*

The output will be the same:

```css
Copy code
Running the main coroutine.
```

In this example, the run_until_complete() method is used to execute the main coroutine within a manually created event loop.

## *Best Practices for Running the Event Loop*

1. **Use asyncio.run()**: For most applications, prefer asyncio.run() for simplicity and ease of use.
2. **Avoid Nesting Loops**: Do not run an event loop within another event loop. This can lead to unexpected behavior and resource leaks.
3. **Clean Up Resources**: Always ensure that the event loop is properly closed after use to free up system resources.

## 3.5 Stopping the Event Loop

Stopping the event loop is an essential part of managing asynchronous tasks in Python. There are several ways to stop the event loop, depending on your use case.

## *Stopping the Event Loop with stop()*

You can stop the event loop programmatically by calling loop.stop(). This method prevents the loop from running any further tasks but does not immediately terminate running tasks.

Example of Stopping the Event Loop

```python
Copy code
import asyncio

async def run_task():
    print("Task started.")
    await asyncio.sleep(3)  # Simulate a long-running task
    print("Task completed.")

async def main():
    task = asyncio.create_task(run_task())
    await asyncio.sleep(1)  # Let the task run for a bit
    print("Stopping the event loop.")
    asyncio.get_running_loop().stop()  # Stop the event loop

asyncio.run(main())
```

## Output Explanation

The output will be:

```arduino
Copy code
Task started.
Stopping the event loop.
```

In this example, the event loop is stopped before the task can complete, demonstrating how to stop execution programmatically.

## Gracefully Stopping the Event Loop

It's important to stop the event loop gracefully to allow any running tasks to complete. You can achieve this by checking for task completion before stopping the loop.

Example of Graceful Stopping

```python
python
Copy code
import asyncio

async def run_task():
    print("Task started.")
    await asyncio.sleep(3)  # Simulate a long-running task
    print("Task completed.")

async def main():
    task = asyncio.create_task(run_task())
    await asyncio.sleep(1)  # Let the task run for a bit
    print("Stopping the event loop.")
    await task  # Wait for the task to complete

asyncio.run(main())
```

## Output Explanation

When you run this code, the output will show that the task completes before stopping:

```arduino
arduino
Copy code
Task started.
Stopping the event loop.
Task completed.
```

In this example, the event loop is stopped only after the task completes, ensuring a graceful shutdown.

## Handling Shutdown Events

You can also handle shutdown events by using loop.add_signal_handler (), allowing you to execute cleanup code before the loop stops. This is particularly useful for applications that need to perform specific actions on exit.

Example of Handling Shutdown Events

```python
Copy code
import asyncio
import signal

async def run_task():
    print("Task started.")
    await asyncio.sleep(3)  # Simulate a long-running task
    print("Task completed.")

def shutdown(loop):
    print("Shutting down the event loop...")
    loop.stop()

async def main():
    loop = asyncio.get_running_loop()
    loop.add_signal_handler(signal.SIGINT, shutdown, loop)  #
    Handle Ctrl+C
    task = asyncio.create_task(run_task())
    await task  # Wait for the task to complete

asyncio.run(main())
```

## Output Explanation

When you run this code and interrupt it with Ctrl+C, the output will be:

```arduino
Copy code
Task started.
^C
Shutting down the event loop...
```

In this example, the event loop is stopped gracefully when a shutdown signal is received, demonstrating how to handle cleanup actions.

## Conclusion

In this chapter, we explored the asyncio event loop in depth. We learned how the event loop operates, how to create and manage it, how to schedule tasks, and how to run and stop it. The event loop is fundamental to asynchronous programming in Python, allowing for efficient execution of I/O-bound operations. Understanding how to leverage the event loop effectively is crucial for building high-performance asynchronous applications.

# Chapter 4: Tasks and Futures

I n this chapter, we will delve into the concepts of tasks and futures within the asyncio library. Understanding how to manage tasks and futures is crucial for building robust asynchronous applications in Python. Tasks and futures provide mechanisms for managing coroutines and handling their results, making it easier to work with concurrent code.

## 4.1 What is a Task?

A task in asyncio is a wrapper for a coroutine, allowing it to run concurrently with other tasks. When you create a task, you schedule a coroutine to be executed by the event loop. Tasks are essential for managing asynchronous operations, as they allow you to track the status of a coroutine and obtain its result or handle exceptions.

### Characteristics of Tasks

- **Concurrent Execution**: Tasks allow multiple coroutines to run concurrently, improving the efficiency of I/O-bound operations.
- **Lifecycle Management**: Tasks have a lifecycle, including states such as pending, running, and completed. This allows you to monitor their progress.
- **Result Retrieval**: Tasks provide a way to retrieve results or exceptions

once they are finished executing.

## Creating a Task

You can create a task using the asyncio.create_task() function, which schedules the coroutine to run in the event loop. The function returns a Task object, which can be used to manage the coroutine.

Example of Creating a Task

```python
Copy code
import asyncio

async def say_hello():
    await asyncio.sleep(1)
    print("Hello, World!")

# Create a task
task = asyncio.create_task(say_hello())

# Wait for the task to complete
asyncio.run(task)
```

## Output Explanation

When you run this code, the output will be:

```
Copy code
Hello, World!
```

In this example, the say_hello coroutine is wrapped in a task and executed within the event loop.

## 4.2 Creating and Managing Tasks

Creating and managing tasks in asyncio involves scheduling coroutines for concurrent execution and monitoring their status.

### *Scheduling Tasks*

You can schedule multiple tasks concurrently using asyncio.create_task() within a coroutine. This allows the event loop to manage the execution of each task independently.

Example of Scheduling Multiple Tasks

```python
Copy code
import asyncio

async def run_task(name, duration):
    print(f"Task {name} starting...")
    await asyncio.sleep(duration)
    print(f"Task {name} completed after {duration} seconds.")

async def main():
    # Schedule multiple tasks
    task1 = asyncio.create_task(run_task("A", 2))
    task2 = asyncio.create_task(run_task("B", 1))
    task3 = asyncio.create_task(run_task("C", 3))

    # Wait for all tasks to complete
    await task1
    await task2
    await task3

asyncio.run(main())
```

## *Output Explanation*

When you run this code, the output will show how tasks run concurrently:

```arduino
Copy code
Task A starting...
Task B starting...
Task C starting...
Task B completed after 1 seconds.
Task A completed after 2 seconds.
Task C completed after 3 seconds.
```

In this example, all three tasks run concurrently, and Task B completes first due to its shorter duration.

## *Managing Task States*

You can check the status of a task using the following properties:

- task.done(): Returns True if the task is completed (either successfully or with an error).
- task.cancelled(): Returns True if the task was canceled.
- task.result(): Retrieves the result of the task if it has completed successfully.
- task.exception(): Retrieves the exception raised by the task if it completed with an error.

### Example of Managing Task States

```python
Copy code
import asyncio

async def run_task(name, duration):
```

```
    await asyncio.sleep(duration)
    return f"Task {name} completed after {duration} seconds."

async def main():
    task = asyncio.create_task(run_task("A", 2))

    await asyncio.sleep(1)  # Allow some time for the task to run
    print(f"Task done? {task.done()}")  # Check if the task is done
    print(f"Task result: {task.result() if task.done() else 'Not
    available yet'}")

    await task  # Wait for the task to complete
    print(f"Task result: {task.result()}")  # Get the result after
    completion

asyncio.run(main())
```

## Output Explanation

When you run this code, the output will be:

```
arduino
Copy code
Task done? False
Task result: Not available yet
Task A completed after 2 seconds.
Task result: Task A completed after 2 seconds.
```

In this example, the task state is checked before and after its completion.

## 4.3 Understanding Futures

A Future is an object that represents a value that may not be available yet. In asyncio, futures are used to handle the results of asynchronous operations, allowing you to check the status of a computation and retrieve its result when it's ready.

## Characteristics of Futures

- **Represents Pending Results**: Futures represent results that are pending, allowing you to work with asynchronous computations.
- **Awaitable**: You can await futures just like you would with coroutines or tasks. When you await a future, your coroutine will pause until the future is done.
- **Callbacks**: You can add callbacks to futures that will be executed when the future is completed, allowing for additional processing.

## Creating a Future

You can create a future using the asyncio.get_running_loop().create_future() method. This allows you to manually control when the future is completed.

Example of Creating and Resolving a Future

```python
Copy code
import asyncio

async def set_future_value(future):
    await asyncio.sleep(1)
    future.set_result("Future resolved!")

async def main():
    loop = asyncio.get_running_loop()
    future = loop.create_future()  # Create a new future

    # Schedule the coroutine that resolves the future
    asyncio.create_task(set_future_value(future))

    result = await future  # Wait for the future to be resolved
    print(result)

asyncio.run(main())
```

## Output Explanation

When you run this code, the output will be:

```
Copy code
Future resolved!
```

In this example, a future is created and resolved by the set_future_value coroutine.

## 4.4 Using asyncio.gather for Concurrency

asyncio.gather() is a powerful utility that allows you to run multiple coroutines concurrently and gather their results. It is particularly useful for executing multiple tasks in parallel and collecting their results in a single call.

### How asyncio.gather() Works

- You pass multiple awaitable objects (coroutines, tasks, or futures) to asyncio.gather().
- The function returns a single awaitable that resolves when all the passed awaitables are done.
- The results are returned as a list, in the order the awaitables were passed.

### Example of Using asyncio.gather()

```python
Copy code
import asyncio

async def run_task(name, duration):
    await asyncio.sleep(duration)
    return f"Task {name} completed after {duration} seconds."
```

```python
async def main():
    results = await asyncio.gather(
        run_task("A", 2),
        run_task("B", 1),
        run_task("C", 3),
    )

    for result in results:
        print(result)

asyncio.run(main())
```

## Output Explanation

When you run this code, the output will show all tasks completed:

```arduino
Copy code
Task B completed after 1 seconds.
Task A completed after 2 seconds.
Task C completed after 3 seconds.
```

In this example, asyncio.gather() runs all tasks concurrently and waits for their completion, allowing you to retrieve their results.

## Handling Exceptions with asyncio.gather()

If any of the tasks passed to asyncio.gather() raises an exception, the entire gather() call will raise that exception. You can handle exceptions by wrapping the call in a try-except block.

Example of Exception Handling with asyncio.gather()

```python
python
Copy code
import asyncio

async def run_task(name, duration):
    await asyncio.sleep(duration)
    if name == "B":
        raise ValueError("An error occurred in Task B!")
    return f"Task {name} completed after {duration} seconds."

async def main():
    try:
        results = await asyncio.gather(
            run_task("A", 2),
            run_task("B", 1),
            run_task("C", 3),
        )
    except ValueError as e:
        print(f"Caught an exception: {e}")
    else:
        for result in results:
            print(result)

asyncio.run(main())
```

## Output Explanation

When you run this code, the output will be:

```arduino
arduino
Copy code
Caught an exception: An error occurred in Task B!
```

In this example, the exception raised in Task B is caught, demonstrating how to handle errors when using asyncio.gather().

## 4.5 Handling Task Results and Exceptions

Handling the results and exceptions of tasks is a crucial aspect of asynchronous programming. By properly managing task outcomes, you can build resilient applications that gracefully handle errors.

### *Retrieving Task Results*

You can retrieve the result of a completed task using the task.result() method. If the task completed successfully, this will return the result. If the task raised an exception, calling this method will raise the same exception.

Example of Retrieving Task Results

```python
Copy code
import asyncio

async def run_task(name, duration):
    await asyncio.sleep(duration)
    return f"Task {name} completed after {duration} seconds."

async def main():
    task = asyncio.create_task(run_task("A", 2))
    await task  # Wait for the task to complete

    # Retrieve the result
    try:
        result = task.result()
        print(result)
    except Exception as e:
        print(f"Task raised an exception: {e}")

asyncio.run(main())
```

## Output Explanation

When you run this code, the output will be:

```arduino
Copy code
Task A completed after 2 seconds.
```

In this example, the result of the task is retrieved and printed after it completes.

## Handling Task Exceptions

You can handle exceptions raised by a task using the try-except block. If you want to wait for multiple tasks and handle exceptions individually, you can use asyncio.gather() with the return_exceptions parameter set to True. This will allow all tasks to run, and their exceptions will be included in the results list.

Example of Handling Exceptions with return_exceptions

```python
Copy code
import asyncio

async def run_task(name, duration):
    await asyncio.sleep(duration)
    if name == "B":
        raise ValueError("An error occurred in Task B!")
    return f"Task {name} completed after {duration} seconds."

async def main():
    results = await asyncio.gather(
        run_task("A", 2),
        run_task("B", 1),
        run_task("C", 3),
```

```
        return_exceptions=True,  # Handle exceptions gracefully
    )

    for result in results:
        if isinstance(result, Exception):
            print(f"Caught an exception: {result}")
        else:
            print(result)

asyncio.run(main())
```

## Output Explanation

When you run this code, the output will be:

```
arduino
Copy code
Caught an exception: An error occurred in Task B!
Task A completed after 2 seconds.
Task C completed after 3 seconds.
```

In this example, the exception raised in Task B is caught and handled, while the other tasks complete successfully.

## Conclusion

In this chapter, we explored tasks and futures in asyncio, learning how to create, manage, and retrieve results from asynchronous tasks. We also covered how to handle exceptions gracefully and use asyncio.gather() for concurrent execution. Understanding tasks and futures is essential for building effective asynchronous applications in Python.

# Chapter 5: Working with Asynchronous I/O

synchronous I/O is a powerful feature of the asyncio library that allows programs to handle I/O-bound tasks efficiently without blocking the execution of other tasks. This chapter will explore various aspects of asynchronous I/O in Python, including file operations, network programming, and implementing a simple web server.

## 5.1 Introduction to Asynchronous I/O

Asynchronous I/O enables programs to perform input/output operations without waiting for them to complete before moving on to the next task. This is particularly useful for I/O-bound applications, where the time spent waiting for I/O operations to complete can be significant.

### Key Benefits of Asynchronous I/O

- **Non-Blocking Execution**: Asynchronous I/O allows other tasks to run while waiting for I/O operations to complete, improving the overall efficiency of applications.
- **Better Resource Utilization**: By allowing concurrent execution, asynchronous I/O can better utilize system resources, particularly in I/O-

heavy applications such as web servers and data processing pipelines.
- **Simplified Concurrency**: Using asyncio, developers can write asynchronous code that is easier to read and maintain compared to traditional threading or multiprocessing models.

## Use Cases for Asynchronous I/O

- **Web Scraping**: Fetching data from multiple web pages concurrently.
- **Networking Applications**: Building chat servers, HTTP clients, or any application that requires network communication.
- **File Processing**: Handling multiple file read/write operations simultaneously.

## 5.2 Using asyncio for File Operations

In addition to networking, asyncio provides a framework for performing asynchronous file operations. While the built-in file handling in Python is synchronous, you can use aiofiles, an external library, to handle file operations asynchronously.

## Installing aiofiles

To use asynchronous file operations, you need to install the aiofiles library. You can do this using pip:

```bash
Copy code
pip install aiofiles
```

## Reading Files Asynchronously

You can read files asynchronously using aiofiles. This allows other tasks to run while the file is being read.

Example of Asynchronous File Reading

```python
Copy code
import aiofiles
import asyncio

async def read_file(filename):
    async with aiofiles.open(filename, mode='r') as file:
        contents = await file.read()
        return contents

async def main():
    content = await read_file('example.txt')
    print(content)

asyncio.run(main())
```

## Output Explanation

In this example, read_file() is an asynchronous function that opens a file and reads its contents without blocking the execution of other tasks. The contents of the file are printed after the read operation is complete.

## Writing Files Asynchronously

Similar to reading files, you can also write to files asynchronously using aiofiles.

Example of Asynchronous File Writing

```python
Copy code
import aiofiles
import asyncio

async def write_file(filename, content):
    async with aiofiles.open(filename, mode='w') as file:
        await file.write(content)

async def main():
    await write_file('output.txt', 'Hello, Async File!')
    print("File written successfully.")

asyncio.run(main())
```

## Output Explanation

When you run this code, the message "File written successfully." is printed after writing to the file asynchronously. This demonstrates how to perform file write operations without blocking other tasks.

## 5.3 Network Programming with asyncio

asyncio is particularly well-suited for network programming, allowing developers to create networked applications that can handle multiple connections concurrently. This is useful for building servers and clients for protocols such as HTTP, FTP, or any custom TCP/UDP protocol.

## Creating a Simple TCP Server

You can create a simple TCP server using the asyncio.start_server() function. This function starts a server that listens for incoming connections and handles them asynchronously.

Example of a Simple TCP Server

```python
Copy code
import asyncio

async def handle_client(reader, writer):
    data = await reader.read(100)
    message = data.decode()
    print(f"Received message: {message}")
    writer.write(data)  # Echo the received message back
    await writer.drain()  # Ensure the data is sent
    writer.close()  # Close the connection

async def main():
    server = await asyncio.start_server(handle_client,
    '127.0.0.1', 8888)
    async with server:
        await server.serve_forever()

asyncio.run(main())
```

## Output Explanation

This TCP server listens for incoming connections on localhost at port 8888. When a client sends a message, the server echoes it back. The handle_client function handles each connection, reading data from the client and writing a response.

## Creating a Simple TCP Client

To interact with the server, you can create a simple TCP client.
  Example of a Simple TCP Client

```python
python
Copy code
import asyncio

async def send_message(message):
    reader, writer = await asyncio.open_connection('127.0.0.1',
    8888)
    print(f"Sending: {message}")
    writer.write(message.encode())
    await writer.drain()  # Ensure the data is sent

    data = await reader.read(100)
    print(f"Received: {data.decode()}")

    writer.close()

async def main():
    await send_message('Hello, Server!')

asyncio.run(main())
```

## Output Explanation

When you run this client, it sends a message to the TCP server and prints the response. This demonstrates how to establish connections and communicate with a server asynchronously.

## 5.4 Asynchronous HTTP Requests

For working with HTTP, aiohttp is a popular library that provides asynchronous HTTP client and server capabilities. You can use aiohttp to perform non-blocking HTTP requests and build asynchronous web applications.

## Installing aiohttp

To use aiohttp, you need to install it via pip:

```bash
Copy code
pip install aiohttp
```

## Making Asynchronous HTTP Requests

With aiohttp, you can make asynchronous HTTP requests easily. The library provides an async with context manager to handle session management.

Example of Making Asynchronous GET Requests

```python
Copy code
import aiohttp
import asyncio

async def fetch(url):
    async with aiohttp.ClientSession() as session:
        async with session.get(url) as response:
            return await response.text()

async def main():
    url = 'https://api.github.com'
    html = await fetch(url)
    print(html)

asyncio.run(main())
```

## Output Explanation

In this example, the fetch() function sends a GET request to the specified URL and retrieves the response asynchronously. The HTML content returned by the server is printed after the request is complete.

## Making Asynchronous POST Requests

You can also make POST requests with aiohttp.

Example of Making Asynchronous POST Requests

```python
Copy code
import aiohttp
import asyncio

async def post_data(url, data):
    async with aiohttp.ClientSession() as session:
        async with session.post(url, json=data) as response:
            return await response.json()

async def main():
    url = 'https://httpbin.org/post'
    data = {'key': 'value'}
    response = await post_data(url, data)
    print(response)

asyncio.run(main())
```

## Output Explanation

When you run this code, it sends a JSON payload to the specified URL and prints the response. This demonstrates how to handle asynchronous POST requests.

## 5.5 Implementing a Simple Web Server

Using aiohttp, you can also implement a simple web server that responds to HTTP requests. This allows you to build asynchronous web applications easily.

### *Creating an Asynchronous Web Server*

Here's how to set up a basic web server using aiohttp.
  Example of a Simple Web Server

```python
Copy code
from aiohttp import web

async def handle(request):
    return web.Response(text="Hello, Async Web!")

app = web.Application()
app.router.add_get('/', handle)

if __name__ == '__main__':
    web.run_app(app, port=8080)
```

### *Output Explanation*

This web server listens for GET requests on the root path (/) and responds with the text "Hello, Async Web!". You can run this server and access it by navigating to http://localhost:8080 in your web browser.

## Handling Different Routes

You can add multiple routes to your web server to handle different paths.
  Example of Handling Multiple Routes

```python
Copy code
from aiohttp import web

async def handle_hello(request):
    return web.Response(text="Hello, Async Web!")

async def handle_goodbye(request):
    return web.Response(text="Goodbye, Async Web!")

app = web.Application()
app.router.add_get('/', handle_hello)
app.router.add_get('/goodbye', handle_goodbye)

if __name__ == '__main__':
    web.run_app(app, port=8080)
```

## Output Explanation

In this example, the web server has two routes: / and /goodbye. Each route returns a different response when accessed. You can test both routes in your web browser.

# Conclusion

In this chapter, we explored various aspects of asynchronous I/O in Python using the asyncio library. We learned how to perform asynchronous file operations using aiofiles, how to create TCP servers and clients for network programming, and how to make asynchronous HTTP requests with aiohttp. Finally, we implemented a simple web server, demonstrating the power of asynchronous programming in building responsive applications.

# Chapter 6: Synchronization Primitives

I n asynchronous programming, multiple tasks may need to share resources or coordinate their execution to prevent race conditions and ensure data consistency. Synchronization primitives in asyncio provide mechanisms for safely sharing resources among asynchronous tasks. In this chapter, we will explore various synchronization primitives available in asyncio, including locks, semaphores, events, and condition variables.

## 6.1 Introduction to Synchronization

Synchronization is essential in concurrent programming to control access to shared resources. In traditional threading, synchronization mechanisms like mutexes and semaphores prevent multiple threads from accessing shared data simultaneously. In asynchronous programming, synchronization serves a similar purpose, ensuring that tasks cooperate correctly when accessing shared resources.

### Key Concepts in Synchronization

- **Race Conditions**: Occur when two or more tasks access shared data simultaneously, leading to unpredictable results.
- **Critical Sections**: Parts of code that access shared resources must be executed by only one task at a time.

- **Blocking vs. Non-Blocking**: Traditional synchronization primitives can block execution, while asynchronous primitives are designed to work without blocking the event loop.

## 6.2 Using Locks in Asyncio

Locks are one of the simplest synchronization primitives. In asyncio, the asyncio.Lock class provides a mechanism for ensuring that only one coroutine can access a critical section at a time.

### *Creating and Using an Asyncio Lock*

Example of Using an Asyncio Lock

```python
Copy code
import asyncio

class SharedResource:
    def __init__(self):
        self.value = 0
        self.lock = asyncio.Lock()

    async def increment(self):
        async with self.lock:
            current_value = self.value
            await asyncio.sleep(1)  # Simulate some processing
            self.value = current_value + 1
            print(f"Value incremented to: {self.value}")

async def main():
    resource = SharedResource()
    tasks = [resource.increment() for _ in range(5)]
    await asyncio.gather(*tasks)

asyncio.run(main())
```

## Output Explanation

In this example, we create a shared resource that has a value and a lock. The increment() method increments the value while holding the lock. Even though we start five tasks that attempt to increment the value concurrently, the lock ensures that only one task can modify the value at a time, preventing race conditions.

# 6.3 Semaphores and Bounded Semaphores

Semaphores are more flexible than locks. They allow a limited number of tasks to access a shared resource simultaneously. This is useful when you want to limit the number of concurrent accesses to a resource, such as a connection pool.

## Creating and Using Semaphores

You can create a semaphore using asyncio.Semaphore, which takes a maximum count as an argument.

Example of Using a Semaphore

```python
Copy code
import asyncio

async def access_resource(semaphore, task_id):
    async with semaphore:
        print(f"Task {task_id} is accessing the resource.")
        await asyncio.sleep(2)  # Simulate some work
        print(f"Task {task_id} is releasing the resource.")

async def main():
    semaphore = asyncio.Semaphore(2)  # Allow up to 2 concurrent
    accesses
    tasks = [access_resource(semaphore, i) for i in range(5)]
```

```
    await asyncio.gather(*tasks)

asyncio.run(main())
```

## Output Explanation

In this example, we create a semaphore that allows up to two tasks to access the resource concurrently. The output shows that only two tasks can access the resource simultaneously, while the others wait until a spot is available.

## Bounded Semaphores

A bounded semaphore is a variation of the semaphore that has a maximum limit on how many times it can be released. This helps prevent programming errors, such as releasing the semaphore more times than it was acquired.

Example of Using a Bounded Semaphore

```python
Copy code
import asyncio

async def access_resource(sem):
    async with sem:
        print("Resource accessed.")
        await asyncio.sleep(1)

async def main():
    sem = asyncio.BoundedSemaphore(2)
    tasks = [access_resource(sem) for _ in range(5)]
    await asyncio.gather(*tasks)

asyncio.run(main())
```

## *Output Explanation*

In this case, if you try to release the bounded semaphore more times than it was acquired, it will raise a ValueError. This feature is beneficial for catching bugs in complex applications.

## 6.4 Events in Asyncio

An event is a simple synchronization primitive that allows one or more coroutines to wait until a certain condition occurs. Events are useful for signaling between tasks.

## *Creating and Using Events*

You can create an event using asyncio.Event(). Tasks can wait for the event to be set, and once it is set, all waiting tasks are notified.

  Example of Using an Event

```python
Copy code
import asyncio

async def waiter(event):
    print("Waiting for the event to be set...")
    await event.wait()  # Wait until the event is set
    print("Event has been set! Continuing execution.")

async def main():
    event = asyncio.Event()
    asyncio.create_task(waiter(event))

    await asyncio.sleep(2)  # Simulate some delay
    print("Setting the event.")
    event.set()  # Set the event

asyncio.run(main())
```

## Output Explanation

In this example, the waiter() coroutine waits for the event to be set. The main() coroutine simulates a delay before setting the event. When the event is set, the waiting task resumes execution.

# 6.5 Condition Variables

Condition variables are more complex synchronization primitives that allow tasks to wait for certain conditions to be met. They are useful in scenarios where one or more tasks need to wait for another task to complete a certain action.

## Creating and Using Condition Variables

You can create a condition variable using asyncio.Condition(). Tasks can wait for the condition to be notified.

Example of Using a Condition Variable

```python
Copy code
import asyncio

class ProducerConsumer:
    def __init__(self):
        self.queue = []
        self.condition = asyncio.Condition()

    async def producer(self):
        async with self.condition:
            for i in range(5):
                self.queue.append(i)
                print(f"Produced {i}")
                self.condition.notify()  # Notify a waiting
                consumer
```

```python
                    await asyncio.sleep(1)

    async def consumer(self):
        async with self.condition:
            while True:
                if not self.queue:
                    print("Queue is empty. Waiting for items...")
                    await self.condition.wait()  # Wait for the
                    producer
                item = self.queue.pop(0)
                print(f"Consumed {item}")

async def main():
    pc = ProducerConsumer()
    await asyncio.gather(pc.producer(), pc.consumer())

asyncio.run(main())
```

## Output Explanation

In this example, we create a producer-consumer model using a condition variable. The producer adds items to the queue and notifies the consumer when an item is produced. The consumer waits for items to be available and consumes them when they are present.

## Conclusion

In this chapter, we explored various synchronization primitives available in asyncio, including locks, semaphores, events, and condition variables. Understanding these primitives is crucial for managing shared resources in asynchronous applications and ensuring that tasks cooperate correctly.

In the next chapter, we will dive deeper into advanced asynchronous programming techniques, including error handling, debugging asynchronous code, and performance optimization strategies.

# Chapter 7: Asynchronous Programming Patterns

Asynchronous programming involves more than just using async and await. In this chapter, we will explore common patterns and techniques used in asynchronous programming with asyncio. We will cover error handling, debugging, and performance optimization strategies to help you write efficient and maintainable asynchronous code.

## 7.1 Error Handling in Asyncio

Handling errors in asynchronous programming can be challenging due to the non-linear execution of tasks. However, using the right patterns can simplify error management.

### Using Try-Except Blocks

You can use try-except blocks in coroutines to handle exceptions gracefully. Any exception raised within an async function can be caught just like in synchronous code.

Example of Error Handling with Try-Except

```python
Copy code
import asyncio

async def risky_task():
    raise ValueError("Something went wrong!")

async def main():
    try:
        await risky_task()
    except ValueError as e:
        print(f"Caught an error: {e}")

asyncio.run(main())
```

71

## Output Explanation

In this example, the exception raised in risky_task() is caught in the main() function. This allows the program to handle errors without crashing.

## Handling Exceptions in Gathered Tasks

When using asyncio.gather(), exceptions in tasks can propagate to the main coroutine. You can also handle them individually.

Example of Handling Exceptions in Gathered Tasks

```python
Copy code
import asyncio

async def task_with_error():
    raise RuntimeError("Task failed!")

async def main():
    tasks = [task_with_error(), asyncio.sleep(1)]
    try:
        await asyncio.gather(*tasks)
    except RuntimeError as e:
        print(f"Caught an error: {e}")

asyncio.run(main())
```

## Output Explanation

In this case, the error raised by one of the tasks is caught in the main() coroutine, demonstrating how to manage exceptions in gathered tasks.

## 7.2 Debugging Asynchronous Code

Debugging asynchronous code can be tricky due to the concurrent execution of tasks. However, asyncio provides tools to help with debugging.

### *Using Print Statements*

The simplest way to debug asynchronous code is to use print statements to track the flow of execution.

Example of Debugging with Print Statements

```python
Copy code
import asyncio

async def task(name):
    print(f"Task {name} started")
    await asyncio.sleep(1)
    print(f"Task {name} finished")

async def main():
    await asyncio.gather(task('A'), task('B'))

asyncio.run(main())
```

### *Using Logging*

The logging module can be used for more advanced debugging. It allows you to control the logging level and format.

Example of Using Logging

```python
Copy code
import asyncio
import logging
```

```python
logging.basicConfig(level=logging.INFO)

async def task(name):
    logging.info(f"Task {name} started")
    await asyncio.sleep(1)
    logging.info(f"Task {name} finished")

async def main():
    await asyncio.gather(task('A'), task('B'))

asyncio.run(main())
```

## Using Debug Mode

You can enable the asyncio debug mode to get additional logging and error reporting, which helps identify issues in your asynchronous code.

Example of Enabling Debug Mode

```python
python
Copy code
import asyncio

asyncio.set_event_loop_policy(asyncio.WindowsSelectorEventLoopPolicy())
 # Needed for Windows
asyncio.run(main(), debug=True)
```

## 7.3 Performance Optimization Strategies

Asynchronous programming can significantly improve performance, but it's important to follow best practices to get the most out of it.

## Use Appropriate Synchronization Primitives

Choosing the right synchronization primitive is crucial. Use locks when you need exclusive access, semaphores for limited resource access, and events or conditions for signaling.

## Avoid Blocking Operations

Ensure that your asynchronous code does not call blocking functions, as this will halt the event loop and negate the benefits of asynchronous programming.

## Use Asynchronous Libraries

When performing I/O-bound operations, use libraries designed for asynchronous programming. For example, use aiohttp for HTTP requests and aiofiles for file operations.

## Profile Your Code

Use profiling tools to identify bottlenecks in your asynchronous code. This helps you understand where optimizations are needed.

## Example of Profiling with cProfile

You can use Python's built-in cProfile module to profile your asynchronous code.

```python
Copy code
import asyncio
import cProfile

async def main():
```

```
    await asyncio.gather(task('A'), task('B'))

if __name__ == '__main__':
    cProfile.run('asyncio.run(main())')
```

## Conclusion

In this chapter, we explored various patterns and techniques for effective asynchronous programming with asyncio. We discussed error handling, debugging strategies, and performance optimization. Understanding these concepts is essential for writing efficient, maintainable, and robust asynchronous applications.

# Chapter 6: Synchronization Primitives

Asynchronous programming enables efficient multitasking by allowing multiple tasks to run concurrently without blocking the execution thread. However, when multiple tasks interact with shared resources, synchronization becomes critical to prevent race conditions and ensure data consistency.

4o mini

You said:

Chapter 7: Asynchronous Context Managers 7.1 What is an Asynchronous Context Manager? 7.2 Creating Asynchronous Context Managers 7.3 Using async with 7.4 Practical Examples of Async Context Managers

ChatGPT said:

ChatGPT

## Chapter 7: Asynchronous Context Managers

Asynchronous context managers provide a convenient way to manage resources and ensure proper setup and teardown of operations in an asynchronous environment. They are particularly useful for handling resources such as files, network connections, or database sessions, where resource management is critical to avoid leaks and ensure that tasks complete without leaving behind dangling resources. This chapter will explore what asynchronous context managers are, how to create them, how to use them, and some practical examples.

## 7.1 What is an Asynchronous Context Manager?

An asynchronous context manager is an object that defines a runtime context to be established when the async with statement is used. Just like regular context managers, which are used with the with statement for synchronous code, asynchronous context managers ensure that specific actions are taken at the beginning and end of a block of code.

### Key Features of Asynchronous Context Managers

- **Setup and Teardown**: They allow for a resource to be acquired and released in a controlled manner.
- **Non-blocking**: They work seamlessly within the async programming model, allowing other tasks to run while waiting for the resource.
- **Integration with async with**: They provide a cleaner syntax for resource management in asynchronous code.

### Example of Context Manager Syntax

Here is the basic syntax of a context manager:

```python
Copy code
async with async_context_manager() as resource:
    # Use the resource
```

In this example, the async_context_manager is an instance of an asynchronous context manager, and resource is the resource obtained for use within the block.

## 7.2 Creating Asynchronous Context Managers

To create an asynchronous context manager, you can define a class with two special methods: __aenter__() and __aexit__(). The __aenter__() method is executed when entering the context, and __aexit__() is executed when exiting the context.

### *Example of Creating an Asynchronous Context Manager*

```python
Copy code
import asyncio

class AsyncResource:
    def __init__(self, name):
        self.name = name

    async def __aenter__(self):
        print(f"{self.name} is being acquired.")
        await asyncio.sleep(1)  # Simulate an asynchronous
        operation
        return self

    async def __aexit__(self, exc_type, exc_val, exc_tb):
        print(f"{self.name} is being released.")
        await asyncio.sleep(1)  # Simulate cleanup operation

async def main():
    async with AsyncResource("Resource A") as resource:
        print(f"Using {resource.name}")

asyncio.run(main())
```

## Output Explanation

In this example, AsyncResource is an asynchronous context manager that simulates acquiring and releasing a resource. When async with is used, the following happens:

1. The __aenter__() method is called, where the resource is acquired.
2. The code block inside the async with statement is executed.
3. Finally, the __aexit__() method is called to release the resource.

The output will demonstrate the sequential flow of acquiring the resource, using it, and then releasing it.

## 7.3 Using async with

Using async with allows you to manage resources more cleanly and avoid boilerplate code associated with manual resource management. The async with statement automatically takes care of entering and exiting the context, making it easier to write robust asynchronous code.

### Benefits of Using async with

- **Simplified Syntax**: Reduces the need for repetitive code for resource management.
- **Automatic Cleanup**: Ensures resources are released even if an error occurs within the block.
- **Better Readability**: Enhances the clarity of the code structure, making it easier to follow.

### Example of Using async with

```python
Copy code
import asyncio

async def process_data():
    async with AsyncResource("Data Processor") as resource:
        # Simulate data processing
        print(f"Processing data with {resource.name}")
        await asyncio.sleep(2)

asyncio.run(process_data())
```

## Output Explanation

This example demonstrates the use of async with for resource management during data processing. The output will show the acquisition of the resource, the processing action, and the eventual release of the resource. If an error were to occur during data processing, the __aexit__() method would still ensure that the resource is released properly.

## 7.4 Practical Examples of Async Context Managers

### Example 1: Asynchronous File Operations

Asynchronous context managers are especially useful in file operations to ensure files are opened and closed correctly without blocking the event loop.
  Asynchronous File Manager Example

```python
Copy code
import aiofiles
import asyncio

class AsyncFile:
```

```python
    def __init__(self, file_name, mode):
        self.file_name = file_name
        self.mode = mode

    async def __aenter__(self):
        self.file = await aiofiles.open(self.file_name, self.mode)
        return self.file

    async def __aexit__(self, exc_type, exc_val, exc_tb):
        await self.file.close()
async def read_file():
    async with AsyncFile("example.txt", "r") as file:
        content = await file.read()
        print(content)

asyncio.run(read_file())
```

## Output Explanation

In this example, the AsyncFile class manages opening and closing a file asynchronously. The aiofiles library is used to handle file operations without blocking. The output will show the content of the file if it exists.

## Example 2: Database Connections

Asynchronous context managers are also valuable for managing database connections, ensuring that connections are opened and closed appropriately.
  Asynchronous Database Connection Example

```python
python
Copy code
import asyncio

class AsyncDatabaseConnection:
```

```python
    def __init__(self, db_url):
        self.db_url = db_url

    async def __aenter__(self):
        print(f"Connecting to database at {self.db_url}.")
        await asyncio.sleep(1)  # Simulate connection time
        return self  # Return the connection object

    async def __aexit__(self, exc_type, exc_val, exc_tb):
        print(f"Closing database connection at {self.db_url}.")
        await asyncio.sleep(1)  # Simulate cleanup time

async def query_database():
    async with AsyncDatabaseConnection("sqlite:///:memory:") as
    connection:
        print("Querying database...")

asyncio.run(query_database())
```

## Output Explanation

In this example, the AsyncDatabaseConnection class simulates managing a database connection. The output will demonstrate the connection being established, a query being simulated, and the connection being closed afterward.

## Conclusion

Asynchronous context managers provide a powerful and convenient way to manage resources in asynchronous programming. By using the async with statement, you can ensure proper setup and teardown of resources while keeping your code clean and readable. In this chapter, we covered the fundamentals of asynchronous context managers, how to create and use them, and explored practical examples.

# Chapter 8: Error Handling and Debugging

A synchronous programming introduces complexity that can lead to unique errors and challenges not typically encountered in synchronous code. Proper error handling and debugging strategies are essential to ensure that your asyncio applications run smoothly and maintainability remains high. In this chapter, we will explore common errors in asynchronous programming, debugging techniques for asyncio code, the use of logging, and best practices for error handling.

## 8.1 Common Errors in Asynchronous Programming

While working with asynchronous code, developers often encounter specific types of errors that stem from the concurrency model. Understanding these common errors is the first step toward effectively handling them.

### 8.1.1 Race Conditions

**Race conditions** occur when two or more tasks access shared data or resources concurrently, leading to unpredictable results. This can happen when tasks are not properly synchronized.

Example of Race Condition

```python
python
Copy code
import asyncio

counter = 0

async def increment():
    global counter
    for _ in range(10000):
        counter += 1

async def main():
    await asyncio.gather(increment(), increment())

asyncio.run(main())
print(counter)  # The result may vary due to race condition
```

In this example, the value of counter may not equal 20000 due to concurrent modifications by the increment() tasks, demonstrating a race condition.

## 8.1.2 Deadlocks

A **deadlock** occurs when two or more tasks are waiting for each other to release resources, causing all tasks to become stuck.

Example of Deadlock

```python
python
Copy code
import asyncio

lock1 = asyncio.Lock()
lock2 = asyncio.Lock()

async def task_a():
    async with lock1:
        await asyncio.sleep(1)  # Simulate work
        async with lock2:  # Wait for lock2
```

```python
        print("Task A finished.")

async def task_b():
    async with lock2:
        await asyncio.sleep(1)  # Simulate work
        async with lock1:  # Wait for lock1
            print("Task B finished.")

async def main():
    await asyncio.gather(task_a(), task_b())

asyncio.run(main())  # This will cause a deadlock
```

Here, task_a and task_b create a deadlock situation by waiting for each other to release locks.

## 8.1.3 Exception Propagation

Exceptions in asynchronous code may not propagate as expected, leading to silent failures if not properly handled. For example, if an exception occurs in a coroutine that is awaited, it may not be caught unless the coroutine is explicitly awaited.

Example of Exception Handling

```python
python
Copy code
import asyncio

async def task():
    raise ValueError("An error occurred!")

async def main():
    try:
        await task()
    except ValueError as e:
        print(f"Caught an exception: {e}")
```

```
asyncio.run(main())
```

In this example, the exception raised in task() is caught in the main() function.

## 8.2 Debugging Asyncio Code

Debugging asynchronous code can be more challenging than synchronous code due to its non-linear execution flow. However, there are strategies to simplify this process.

### 8.2.1 Using Print Statements

While not the most sophisticated method, adding print statements in strategic locations can help trace the flow of execution in asynchronous code.

```python
python
Copy code
async def task(name):
    print(f"Task {name} started.")
    await asyncio.sleep(1)
    print(f"Task {name} finished.")

async def main():
    await asyncio.gather(task('A'), task('B'))

asyncio.run(main())
```

### 8.2.2 Using the Debugger

Python's built-in debugger (pdb) can be useful for debugging asyncio code. However, you need to be careful about how you set breakpoints since the code execution is concurrent.

Example of Using pdb

```python
Copy code
import asyncio
import pdb

async def task():
    pdb.set_trace()  # Set a breakpoint
    await asyncio.sleep(1)

async def main():
    await task()

asyncio.run(main())
```

## 8.2.3 Enabling Debug Mode in Asyncio

asyncio provides a debug mode that helps catch common errors in asynchronous code. You can enable debug mode with the following:

```python
Copy code
import asyncio

asyncio.run(main(), debug=True)
```

When debug mode is enabled, asyncio will provide detailed error reports and warnings about common issues, making it easier to identify potential problems in your code.

## 8.3 Using Logging in Asyncio Applications

Logging is a powerful tool for diagnosing issues in asynchronous applications. Python's logging module allows for structured logging, which is invaluable when debugging complex asynchronous workflows.

## 8.3.1 Basic Logging Setup

To set up logging in an asyncio application, you can use the following configuration:

```python
Copy code
import logging
import asyncio

logging.basicConfig(level=logging.INFO)

async def task(name):
    logging.info(f"Task {name} started.")
    await asyncio.sleep(1)
    logging.info(f"Task {name} finished.")

async def main():
    await asyncio.gather(task('A'), task('B'))

asyncio.run(main())
```

## 8.3.2 Logging Exceptions

To log exceptions in your asynchronous code, you can use try and except blocks along with logging.

```python
Copy code
async def task_with_error():
    try:
        raise ValueError("An error occurred in the task.")
    except Exception as e:
        logging.error(f"Error in task: {e}")

async def main():
```

```
    await task_with_error()

asyncio.run(main())
```

### 8.3.3 Advanced Logging Configuration

For more complex applications, you may want to configure logging handlers, formats, and levels to better suit your needs.

```python
python
Copy code
logger = logging.getLogger("MyAsyncApp")
handler = logging.FileHandler("app.log")
formatter = logging.Formatter('%(asctime)s - %(levelname)s -
%(message)s')
handler.setFormatter(formatter)
logger.addHandler(handler)
logger.setLevel(logging.INFO)
```

## 8.4 Best Practices for Error Handling

To create robust and maintainable asynchronous applications, it's essential to follow best practices for error handling.

### 8.4.1 Use Exception Handling Wisely

Always handle exceptions explicitly where you anticipate potential failures. Use try and except blocks to catch exceptions and take appropriate actions.

## 8.4.2 Propagate Exceptions as Needed

Sometimes, you may want to propagate exceptions up the call stack. Ensure that you do this by re-raising exceptions in the appropriate context.

```python
Copy code
async def task():
    try:
        raise ValueError("An error occurred!")
    except ValueError:
        logging.error("Handling error.")
        raise  # Propagate the exception
```

## 8.4.3 Avoid Swallowing Exceptions

Be cautious not to inadvertently swallow exceptions by catching broad exceptions (e.g., except Exception as e:) without handling them appropriately. Always handle exceptions specifically.

## 8.4.4 Utilize Built-in Error Handling Tools

Make use of built-in error handling tools provided by asyncio, such as asyncio.gather()'s return_exceptions parameter, which allows you to collect exceptions raised by tasks without halting execution.

```python
Copy code
async def task_with_exception():
    raise ValueError("An error occurred!")

async def main():
    results = await asyncio.gather(task_with_exception(),
    return_exceptions=True)
    print(results)  # [ValueError("An error occurred!")]
```

## 8.4.5 Log Critical Errors

Implement logging for critical errors that require attention. This helps in identifying recurring issues and aids in debugging.

# Conclusion

In this chapter, we explored the intricacies of error handling and debugging in asynchronous programming with asyncio. We discussed common errors, effective debugging techniques, and the importance of logging in identifying issues. By following best practices for error handling, you can create robust asynchronous applications that are easier to maintain and debug.

# Chapter 9: Advanced Topics

Asynchronous programming with asyncio allows developers to write efficient, non-blocking applications. However, to fully leverage its capabilities, it's essential to understand advanced topics that go beyond the basics. This chapter covers custom event loops, integrating asyncio with other libraries, combining asyncio with threading and multiprocessing, performance optimization, and using asyncio for real-time applications.

## 9.1 Custom Event Loops

The default event loop provided by asyncio is sufficient for most applications, but there may be cases where creating a custom event loop is necessary. A custom event loop can provide specific functionality or integrate with different I/O models.

### 9.1.1 Creating a Custom Event Loop

To create a custom event loop, you can subclass asyncio.AbstractEventLoop and implement the required methods. Here's an example of a simple custom event loop:

```python
python
Copy code
import asyncio

class CustomEventLoop(asyncio.AbstractEventLoop):
    def __init__(self):
        super().__init__()
        self._ready = []
        self._running = False

    def run(self):
        self._running = True
        while self._ready:
            task = self._ready.pop(0)
            task()  # Run the task

    def call_soon(self, callback, *args):
        self._ready.append(lambda: callback(*args))

    def stop(self):
        self._running = False

async def simple_task():
    print("Task executed.")

def main():
    loop = CustomEventLoop()
    loop.call_soon(simple_task)
    loop.run()

main()
```

## 9.1.2 Overriding Default Methods

When creating a custom event loop, it is crucial to override default methods, such as run, stop, and call_soon. This allows you to define how tasks are scheduled and executed within your custom loop.

## 9.2 Running Asyncio with Other Libraries

asyncio can be integrated with various libraries to enhance functionality and support more complex use cases. Libraries like aiohttp for HTTP requests and aiomysql for asynchronous database interactions are commonly used.

### 9.2.1 Using aiohttp for Asynchronous HTTP Requests

aiohttp is an asynchronous HTTP client and server framework that allows you to perform non-blocking HTTP requests.

Example of Asynchronous HTTP Request with aiohttp

```python
Copy code
import aiohttp
import asyncio

async def fetch(url):
    async with aiohttp.ClientSession() as session:
        async with session.get(url) as response:
            return await response.text()

async def main():
    content = await fetch('https://www.example.com')
    print(content)

asyncio.run(main())
```

### 9.2.2 Using aiomysql for Asynchronous Database Operations

aiomysql is an asynchronous MySQL driver for asyncio. It allows you to execute SQL queries without blocking the event loop.

Example of Asynchronous Database Operation with aiomysql

```python
Copy code
import aiomysql
import asyncio

async def query_database():
    conn = await aiomysql.connect(host='localhost', port=3306,
    user='user', password='password', db='test_db')
    async with conn.cursor() as cur:
        await cur.execute("SELECT * FROM my_table;")
        result = await cur.fetchall()
        print(result)
    conn.close()

asyncio.run(query_database())
```

## 9.3 Integrating Asyncio with Threading and Multiprocessing

While asyncio provides a powerful framework for concurrent programming, there are scenarios where you may need to integrate it with threading or multiprocessing for CPU-bound tasks.

### 9.3.1 Using Threading with Asyncio

You can use Python's concurrent.futures.ThreadPoolExecutor to run blocking code in a separate thread while using asyncio for the rest of your application.

Example of Using Threading with Asyncio

```python
Copy code
import asyncio
from concurrent.futures import ThreadPoolExecutor

def blocking_io():
```

```python
    # Simulate a blocking I/O operation
    print("Blocking I/O operation starting.")
    import time
    time.sleep(3)
    print("Blocking I/O operation completed.")

async def main():
    loop = asyncio.get_event_loop()
    with ThreadPoolExecutor() as pool:
        await loop.run_in_executor(pool, blocking_io)

asyncio.run(main())
```

## 9.3.2 Using Multiprocessing with Asyncio

For CPU-bound tasks, you can use concurrent.futures.ProcessPoolExecutor to run code in separate processes.

Example of Using Multiprocessing with Asyncio

```python
python
Copy code
import asyncio
from concurrent.futures import ProcessPoolExecutor

def cpu_bound_task():
    # Simulate a CPU-bound operation
    print("CPU-bound operation starting.")
    sum(range(10**6))  # Example computation
    print("CPU-bound operation completed.")

async def main():
    loop = asyncio.get_event_loop()
    with ProcessPoolExecutor() as pool:
        await loop.run_in_executor(pool, cpu_bound_task)

asyncio.run(main())
```

## 9.4 Performance Considerations and Optimization

When working with asyncio, understanding performance considerations is crucial to ensure your applications run efficiently.

### 9.4.1 Reducing Context Switching

Excessive context switching between coroutines can lead to performance degradation. To minimize this, structure your code to allow coroutines to yield control without unnecessary context switches.

### 9.4.2 Limiting Concurrent Tasks

While it's tempting to run many tasks concurrently, excessive concurrency can lead to resource exhaustion. Use tools like asyncio.Semaphore to limit the number of concurrently running tasks.

Example of Limiting Concurrent Tasks

```python
python
Copy code
import asyncio

semaphore = asyncio.Semaphore(5)

async def limited_task(n):
    async with semaphore:
        print(f"Task {n} starting.")
        await asyncio.sleep(1)  # Simulate work
        print(f"Task {n} finished.")

async def main():
    await asyncio.gather(*(limited_task(i) for i in range(10)))

asyncio.run(main())
```

### 9.4.3 Profiling and Monitoring

Use profiling tools to analyze the performance of your asyncio applications. Libraries like aiomonitor can help you monitor the event loop and detect performance bottlenecks.

## 9.5 Using Asyncio for Real-Time Applications

asyncio is particularly well-suited for real-time applications where low latency and responsiveness are critical, such as chat applications, game servers, or IoT systems.

### 9.5.1 Building a Simple Chat Application

A simple chat application can be built using asyncio to handle multiple client connections simultaneously.

Example of a Simple Chat Server

```python
Copy code
import asyncio

clients = set()

async def handle_client(reader, writer):
    clients.add(writer)
    while True:
        data = await reader.read(100)
        if not data:
            break
        message = data.decode()
        print(f"Received: {message}")
        # Broadcast message to all clients
        for client in clients:
            if client != writer:
                client.write(data)
```

```python
        await client.drain()
    clients.remove(writer)
    writer.close()

async def main():
    server = await asyncio.start_server(handle_client,
    '127.0.0.1', 8888)
    print("Chat server started...")
    async with server:
        await server.serve_forever()

asyncio.run(main())
```

## 9.5.2 Real-Time Data Processing

Using asyncio for real-time data processing allows for handling streaming data from various sources efficiently.

Example of Real-Time Data Processing

```python
python
Copy code
import asyncio

async def process_data(source):
    while True:
        data = await source.get()
        print(f"Processing data: {data}")

async def data_producer(queue):
    for i in range(10):
        await asyncio.sleep(0.5)  # Simulate data arrival
        await queue.put(i)

async def main():
    queue = asyncio.Queue()
    await asyncio.gather(data_producer(queue), process_data(queue))
```

```
asyncio.run(main())
```

## Conclusion

In this chapter, we explored advanced topics in asyncio, including creating custom event loops, integrating with other libraries, and combining asyncio with threading and multiprocessing. We also discussed performance considerations and showcased how to use asyncio for real-time applications. Understanding these advanced topics will empower you to write more efficient, responsive, and scalable applications using asynchronous programming with Python.

# Chapter 10: Testing Asynchronous Code

Testing asynchronous code can be challenging due to its non-linear execution flow and the concurrency model. However, with the right tools and practices, you can effectively test your asynchronous applications to ensure they behave as expected. This chapter covers the fundamentals of testing in Python, how to write unit tests for asynchronous code, utilizing pytest with asyncio, mocking and patching in asynchronous tests, and best practices for testing asyncio applications.

## 10.1 Introduction to Testing in Python

Testing is a critical aspect of software development that helps ensure code quality, reliability, and maintainability. Python provides several built-in modules and third-party libraries to facilitate testing.

### 10.1.1 Types of Tests

There are several types of tests you may encounter in Python development:

- **Unit Tests**: Test individual components or functions in isolation.
- **Integration Tests**: Test how different components work together.
- **Functional Tests**: Test the application from an end-user perspective.
- **Performance Tests**: Measure the application's performance under specific conditions.

## 10.1.2 Testing Frameworks

Python has several testing frameworks, with unittest being the built-in option. However, many developers prefer using pytest due to its simplicity and powerful features.

# 10.2 Writing Unit Tests for Async Code

When writing unit tests for asynchronous code, it's important to structure your tests to await the execution of coroutines properly.

## 10.2.1 Basic Unit Test Structure

A basic unit test for an asynchronous function can be structured as follows:

```python
Copy code
import asyncio
import unittest

async def async_function():
    await asyncio.sleep(1)
    return "Hello, World!"

class TestAsyncFunction(unittest.TestCase):
    def test_async_function(self):
        result = asyncio.run(async_function())
        self.assertEqual(result, "Hello, World!")

if __name__ == '__main__':
    unittest.main()
```

In this example, asyncio.run() is used to execute the asynchronous function and obtain the result for assertions.

## 10.2.2 Using unittest.IsolatedAsyncioTestCase

Starting from Python 3.8, the unittest module provides IsolatedAsyncioTest Case, which simplifies testing asynchronous code:

```python
Copy code
import unittest

class TestAsyncFunction(unittest.IsolatedAsyncioTestCase):
    async def test_async_function(self):
        result = await async_function()
        self.assertEqual(result, "Hello, World!")

if __name__ == '__main__':
    unittest.main()
```

## 10.3 Using pytest for Asyncio

pytest is a popular testing framework that simplifies the testing process. It supports asynchronous testing through the pytest-asyncio plugin.

## 10.3.1 Installing pytest-asyncio

To get started with pytest and pytest-asyncio, install the package via pip:

```bash
Copy code
pip install pytest pytest-asyncio
```

## 10.3.2 Writing Async Tests with pytest

You can write asynchronous tests easily using pytest by marking your test functions with @pytest.mark.asyncio:

```python
Copy code
import pytest

@pytest.mark.asyncio
async def test_async_function():
    result = await async_function()
    assert result == "Hello, World!"
```

## 10.3.3 Running pytest

To run your tests, simply execute the following command in your terminal:

```bash
Copy code
pytest
```

This command will discover and run all test functions defined in your project.

# 10.4 Mocking and Patching in Asynchronous Tests

Mocking is a powerful technique that allows you to replace parts of your system under test with mock objects. This is particularly useful in asynchronous tests where you might want to isolate the unit of work.

## 10.4.1 Using unittest.mock

The unittest.mock module provides tools for mocking objects. You can use asyncio-compatible mocks for testing asynchronous functions.

Example of Mocking an Asynchronous Function

```python
Copy code
from unittest import mock

async def fetch_data():
    await asyncio.sleep(1)
    return "data"

async def process_data():
    data = await fetch_data()
    return f"Processed {data}"

@mock.patch('__main__.fetch_data', return_value="mocked data")
async def test_process_data(mock_fetch):
    result = await process_data()
    assert result == "Processed mocked data"
```

In this example, fetch_data is mocked to return a predetermined value, allowing you to test the process_data function without invoking the actual fetch_data logic.

## 10.4.2 Using pytest-mock

pytest-mock is a plugin for pytest that simplifies mocking. It integrates seamlessly with pytest and allows for more straightforward assertions.

Example of Mocking with pytest-mock

```python
Copy code
```

```
import pytest

@pytest.mark.asyncio
async def test_process_data(mocker):
    mocker.patch('__main__.fetch_data', return_value="mocked data")
    result = await process_data()
    assert result == "Processed mocked data"
```

## 10.5 Best Practices for Testing Asyncio Applications

To ensure the reliability and maintainability of your asynchronous applications, follow these best practices when testing:

### 10.5.1 Keep Tests Isolated

Ensure that your tests are isolated from each other. Each test should set up its context and not depend on the results of other tests. This isolation prevents side effects and makes debugging easier.

### 10.5.2 Use Async Assertions

When asserting values in asynchronous tests, ensure you are awaiting the results properly. Use async assertions to confirm the expected outcomes.

### 10.5.3 Test for Exceptions

Make sure to test for expected exceptions in your asynchronous code. Use the pytest.raises context manager or equivalent mechanisms to assert that the correct exceptions are raised.

Example of Testing for Exceptions

```python
python
Copy code
import pytest

async def async_function_with_error():
    raise ValueError("An error occurred!")

@pytest.mark.asyncio
async def test_async_function_with_error():
    with pytest.raises(ValueError) as excinfo:
        await async_function_with_error()
    assert str(excinfo.value) == "An error occurred!"
```

## 10.5.4 Profile Your Tests

For applications that require high performance, consider profiling your tests to identify slow or resource-intensive operations. Use profiling tools to analyze and optimize your test execution.

## 10.5.5 Continuous Integration

Integrate your tests into a continuous integration (CI) pipeline to ensure that your asynchronous code remains functional as changes are made. Tools like GitHub Actions, Travis CI, or Jenkins can automate test execution on code changes.

## Conclusion

Testing asynchronous code is critical for ensuring the reliability and performance of your applications. By understanding how to write unit tests, leverage pytest and its plugins, and use mocking effectively, you can create robust tests for your asynchronous code. Following best practices in testing will further enhance the quality of your applications, making them easier to maintain and extend.

# Chapter 11: Real-World Applications

A synchronous programming with asyncio offers significant advantages in building responsive, efficient applications. This chapter explores real-world applications of asyncio, showcasing how it can be leveraged in various domains such as web development, web scraping, chat applications, and data processing pipelines. We will also review case studies of asyncio in production environments.

## 11.1 Building a RESTful API with FastAPI and Asyncio

FastAPI is a modern web framework for building APIs with Python that is designed to be fast and easy to use. It supports asynchronous programming, making it a perfect fit for applications that require high performance and scalability.

### 11.1.1 Setting Up FastAPI

To get started, first install FastAPI and an ASGI server, such as uvicorn:

```bash
Copy code
pip install fastapi uvicorn
```

## 11.1.2 Creating a Simple API

Here's a simple example of a FastAPI application that provides asynchronous endpoints for managing items:

```python
Copy code
from fastapi import FastAPI

app = FastAPI()

items = {}

@app.post("/items/{item_id}")
async def create_item(item_id: int, item: str):
    items[item_id] = item
    return {"item_id": item_id, "item": item}

@app.get("/items/{item_id}")
async def read_item(item_id: int):
    return {"item_id": item_id, "item": items.get(item_id, "Item
    not found")}

if __name__ == "__main__":
    import uvicorn
    uvicorn.run(app, host="127.0.0.1", port=8000)
```

## 11.1.3 Running the API

Run the API using the following command:

```bash
Copy code
uvicorn main:app --reload
```

You can then interact with the API using tools like curl, Postman, or a web

110

browser.

## 11.1.4 Benefits of Using Asyncio with FastAPI

Using asyncio with FastAPI allows for non-blocking I/O operations, enabling the handling of multiple requests simultaneously. This makes your API scalable and efficient, especially when dealing with high concurrency.

## 11.2 Creating a Web Scraper with Asyncio

Web scraping is a common task that can benefit greatly from asynchronous programming, particularly when fetching multiple pages concurrently.

### 11.2.1 Setting Up the Scraper

You'll need aiohttp for making asynchronous HTTP requests and Beautiful-Soup for parsing HTML. Install these libraries as follows:

```bash
Copy code
pip install aiohttp beautifulsoup4
```

### 11.2.2 Writing the Scraper

Here's an example of a simple asynchronous web scraper that retrieves titles from a list of URLs:

```python
Copy code
import aiohttp
import asyncio
from bs4 import BeautifulSoup
```

```python
async def fetch(url):
    async with aiohttp.ClientSession() as session:
        async with session.get(url) as response:
            return await response.text()

async def scrape_title(url):
    html = await fetch(url)
    soup = BeautifulSoup(html, 'html.parser')
    title = soup.title.string if soup.title else "No title"
    return title

async def main(urls):
    tasks = [scrape_title(url) for url in urls]
    return await asyncio.gather(*tasks)

urls = [
    'https://www.example.com',
    'https://www.python.org',
    'https://www.wikipedia.org',
]

titles = asyncio.run(main(urls))
print(titles)
```

## 11.2.3 Benefits of Asynchronous Scraping

Asynchronous web scraping allows for faster data retrieval since multiple requests are made concurrently, significantly reducing the time required to scrape data from several pages.

## 11.3 Implementing Chat Applications

Chat applications require real-time communication between clients and servers. Using asyncio, you can efficiently manage multiple connections.

## 11.3.1 Building a Simple Chat Server

Here's how to create a basic chat server using asyncio:

```python
Copy code
import asyncio

clients = set()

async def handle_client(reader, writer):
    clients.add(writer)
    while True:
        data = await reader.read(100)
        if not data:
            break
        message = data.decode()
        print(f"Received: {message}")
        for client in clients:
            if client != writer:
                client.write(data)
                await client.drain()
    clients.remove(writer)
    writer.close()

async def main():
    server = await asyncio.start_server(handle_client,
    '127.0.0.1', 8888)
    async with server:
        await server.serve_forever()

asyncio.run(main())
```

## 11.3.2 Client Implementation

You can create a simple client to connect to the chat server:

```python
Copy code
import asyncio

async def chat_client():
    reader, writer = await asyncio.open_connection('127.0.0.1',
    8888)
    while True:
        message = input("Enter message: ")
        writer.write(message.encode())
        await writer.drain()

asyncio.run(chat_client())
```

### 11.3.3 Features of Asynchronous Chat Applications

Asynchronous chat applications can handle multiple clients concurrently, allowing for real-time messaging without blocking operations. This results in a responsive user experience.

## 11.4 Data Processing Pipelines with Asyncio

Data processing pipelines often involve multiple steps, such as fetching data, processing it, and storing the results. Using asyncio can enhance the performance of these pipelines.

### 11.4.1 Example of a Simple Data Pipeline

Below is an example of a data processing pipeline that fetches data, processes it, and outputs the results:

```python
Copy code
```

```
import aiohttp
import asyncio

async def fetch_data(url):
    async with aiohttp.ClientSession() as session:
        async with session.get(url) as response:
            return await response.json()

async def process_data(data):
    # Simulate data processing
    await asyncio.sleep(1)  # Replace with actual processing logic
    return f"Processed {data}"

async def main(urls):
    data = await asyncio.gather(*(fetch_data(url) for url in urls))
    results = await asyncio.gather(*(process_data(item) for item
    in data))
    return results

urls = [
    'https://api.example.com/data1',
    'https://api.example.com/data2',
]

results = asyncio.run(main(urls))
print(results)
```

## 11.4.2 Advantages of Using Asyncio in Data Pipelines

Using asyncio in data processing pipelines enables concurrent fetching and processing of data, significantly improving the overall throughput and efficiency of the pipeline.

## 11.5 Case Studies of Asyncio in Production

Understanding how asyncio is used in real-world applications can provide insights into its practical applications and benefits.

### 11.5.1 Case Study: High-Performance Web Services

Many companies use asyncio to build high-performance web services capable of handling thousands of requests per second. For example, a financial services company might use asyncio to manage real-time data feeds from multiple sources, ensuring that their services remain responsive and up-to-date.

### 11.5.2 Case Study: IoT Applications

In IoT applications, devices often need to communicate with servers to send and receive data. Using asyncio, developers can create scalable solutions that manage numerous device connections efficiently, allowing for real-time data processing and analysis.

### 11.5.3 Case Study: Asynchronous Data Pipelines

Companies that deal with large amounts of data often leverage asyncio to build efficient data processing pipelines. These pipelines can handle tasks like data ingestion, transformation, and loading (ETL) while maintaining high throughput and low latency.

## Conclusion

In this chapter, we explored various real-world applications of asyncio, including building RESTful APIs with FastAPI, creating web scrapers, implementing chat applications, and designing data processing pipelines. We also reviewed case studies that illustrate the practical use of asyncio in production environments. By leveraging asynchronous programming, developers can create efficient, scalable applications that handle high concurrency and deliver superior performance.

# Chapter 12: Conclusion

As we reach the end of our exploration of asynchronous programming with asyncio, it's important to reflect on the key concepts we've covered, discuss the future of asynchronous programming in Python, and provide resources for further learning. Additionally, we'll touch upon the community and opportunities for contribution in the realm of asynchronous programming.

## 12.1 Recap of Key Concepts

Throughout this book, we delved into various facets of asynchronous programming with asyncio. Here's a recap of the key concepts:

- **Asynchronous Programming Fundamentals**: We began with an introduction to asynchronous programming, discussing its importance in creating non-blocking applications that can handle multiple tasks concurrently.
- **Coroutines**: We explored coroutines, the building blocks of asynchronous code, and learned how to define and manage them using the async and await keywords.
- **The Asyncio Event Loop**: Understanding the event loop was crucial, as it is responsible for executing asynchronous tasks. We covered how to create, manage, and run the event loop effectively.

- **Tasks and Futures**: We learned about asyncio tasks and futures, which provide mechanisms for managing concurrent execution and handling results or exceptions from asynchronous operations.
- **Asynchronous I/O**: We examined how asyncio can be used for non-blocking I/O operations, making it suitable for tasks like network programming and file handling.
- **Synchronization Primitives**: We covered various synchronization primitives such as locks, semaphores, and events, which are essential for coordinating access to shared resources in concurrent environments.
- **Asynchronous Context Managers**: The chapter on asynchronous context managers introduced a new way to manage resources asynchronously, improving code readability and ensuring proper cleanup.
- **Error Handling and Debugging**: We discussed common errors in asynchronous programming, strategies for debugging, and best practices for logging and error handling.
- **Advanced Topics**: We explored custom event loops, integrating asyncio with other libraries, and performance considerations, providing insights into optimizing asynchronous applications.
- **Real-World Applications**: Finally, we looked at practical applications of asyncio in building RESTful APIs, web scraping, chat applications, and data processing pipelines, along with case studies showcasing its use in production environments.

## 12.2 Future of Asynchronous Programming in Python

The future of asynchronous programming in Python looks promising. As applications become more complex and demand higher performance, the need for efficient concurrency solutions will continue to grow. Key trends that may shape the future include:

- **Increased Adoption of Async Libraries**: Asynchronous libraries like FastAPI and aiohttp are gaining popularity, providing robust frameworks for building scalable applications.

- **Integration with Other Technologies**: There is a trend toward integrating asynchronous programming with technologies such as WebSockets, microservices, and cloud computing, enhancing the ability to build real-time applications.
- **Enhanced Language Features**: Future versions of Python may introduce new features or enhancements to the asyncio library, making it even easier for developers to write asynchronous code.
- **Broader Community Engagement**: The growth of the Python community around asynchronous programming will likely lead to more tutorials, tools, and libraries that simplify asynchronous development.

## 12.3 Resources for Further Learning

To continue your journey in asynchronous programming with Python, consider the following resources:

1. **Official Python Documentation**: The Python official documentation provides in-depth explanations of the asyncio library and related features.
2. **Books**:

- *"Fluent Python"* by Luciano Ramalho covers asynchronous programming in Python in detail.
- *"Python Concurrency with asyncio"* by Matthew Fowler is a comprehensive guide specifically focused on asyncio.

1. **Online Courses**: Platforms like Coursera, Udemy, and Pluralsight offer courses on asynchronous programming and Python development that can enhance your knowledge and skills.
2. **Blogs and Tutorials**: Websites like Real Python, Medium, and Dev.to frequently publish articles and tutorials on asyncio and related topics.
3. **YouTube Channels**: Channels like Corey Schafer and Tech With Tim offer video tutorials on Python and asynchronous programming

concepts.

## 12.4 Community and Contribution

Engaging with the community is a valuable way to learn and share knowledge. Here are some ways to get involved:

- **Forums and Discussion Groups**: Join communities such as Stack Overflow, Reddit's r/Python, or the Python Discord server to ask questions, share experiences, and connect with other developers.
- **Open Source Contributions**: Contributing to open-source projects that utilize asyncio can help you gain practical experience. Check platforms like GitHub for projects seeking contributors.
- **Attend Meetups and Conferences**: Participate in local or virtual meetups and conferences focused on Python and asynchronous programming. These events are excellent for networking and learning from industry experts.
- **Write and Share**: Consider writing articles or creating tutorials on your experiences with asyncio. Sharing knowledge helps the community grow and reinforces your own understanding.

## Conclusion

Asynchronous programming with asyncio opens up a world of possibilities for building efficient and scalable applications in Python. By mastering the concepts presented in this book, you can harness the power of asyncio to tackle complex problems and create responsive, high-performance applications.